Sniff, Sniff

A Book About Smell

Thanks to our advisers for their expertise, research, and advice:

Angela Busch, M.D.
All About Children Pediatrics
Minneapolis, Minnesota

Susan Kesselring, M.A.
Literacy Educator
Rosemount-Apple Valley-Eagan
(Minnesota) School District

PICTURE WINDOW BOOKS
Minneapolis, Minnesota

by Dana Meachen Rau

illustrated by Rick Peterson

Managing Editor: Catherine Neitge
Creative Director: Terri Foley
Art Director: Keith Griffin
Editor: Christianne Jones
Designer: Nathan Gassman
Page Production: Picture Window Books
The illustrations in this book are gouache paintings.

Picture Window Books
5115 Excelsior Boulevard
Suite 232
Minneapolis, MN 55416
877-845-8392
www.picturewindowbooks.com

Printed in the United States of America.

Library of Congress Cataloging-in-Publication Data
Rau, Dana Meachen, 1971-
Sniff, sniff : a book about smell / by Dana Meachen
Rau ; illustrated by Rick Peterson.
p. cm. — (Amazing body)
Includes bibliographical references and index.
ISBN 1-4048-1020-X (hardcover)
1. Smell—Juvenile literature. 2. Nose—Juvenile
literature. I. Peterson, Rick. II. Title. III. Series.

QP458.R38 2005
612.8'6—dc22   2004019170

A delicious smell floats into your room and wakes you up. Breakfast must be ready.

Your sense of smell is one of your five senses. It helps you tell the difference between a good smell like cinnamon toast and a bad smell like burnt toast.

Smells in the air are called **odors.**

Take a big sniff with your nose. You can feel air going into your nostrils. Your body needs air to live. Taking in and letting out air through your nose is called breathing.

When you breathe in, the odors in the air enter your nose. Every time you breathe, you are smelling the air.

When you breathe, nose hairs clean the air as it enters your body.

Smaller hairs way in the back of your nose also clean the air. These tiny hairs are called cilia.

Dirt and dust in the air get stuck to your nose hairs. The hairs keep the dirt and dust from getting into your lungs.

There is also a sticky substance inside your nose. It is called mucus.

mucus

nose hair

nostril

Mucus helps trap odors, dirt, and dust. You can see what mucus looks like when you blow your nose.

11

After the air passes through the hair and mucus, it reaches nerve cells in the upper part of your nose. These cells have nerves that are connected to the brain.

Nerves are tiny cords that run through your whole body.

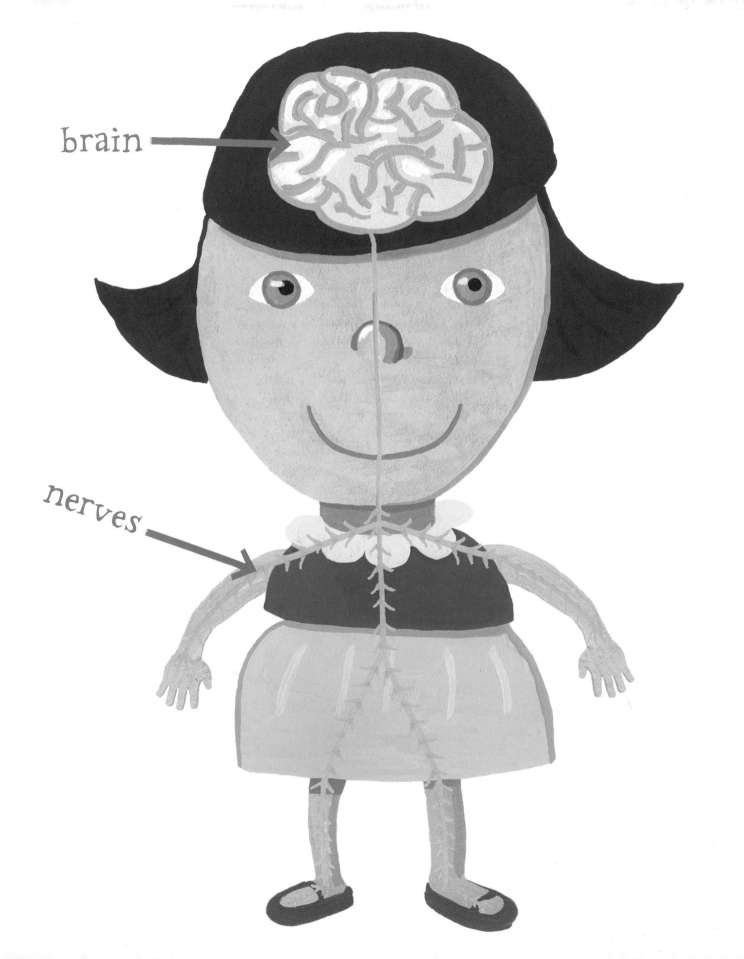

brain

nerves

13

When you smell an odor, your nerve cells send a message to your brain.

Your brain lets you know
what you are smelling.

After a while, you may not notice a smell anymore.

STINKY

Your body
gets used
to it.
Your brain
stops thinking
about it.

Your sense of smell can keep you safe. The smell of gasoline or bleach can sting your nose. That is your body's way of telling you something is dangerous.

Smelling smoke can warn you of a fire.

Take a deep breath. Now what do you smell?

Whether the smell is good or bad, your sense of smell is hard at work.

Your sense of smell and sense of taste are closely related. When you have a cold and your nose is filled with mucus, it is often very hard to taste what you eat and drink.

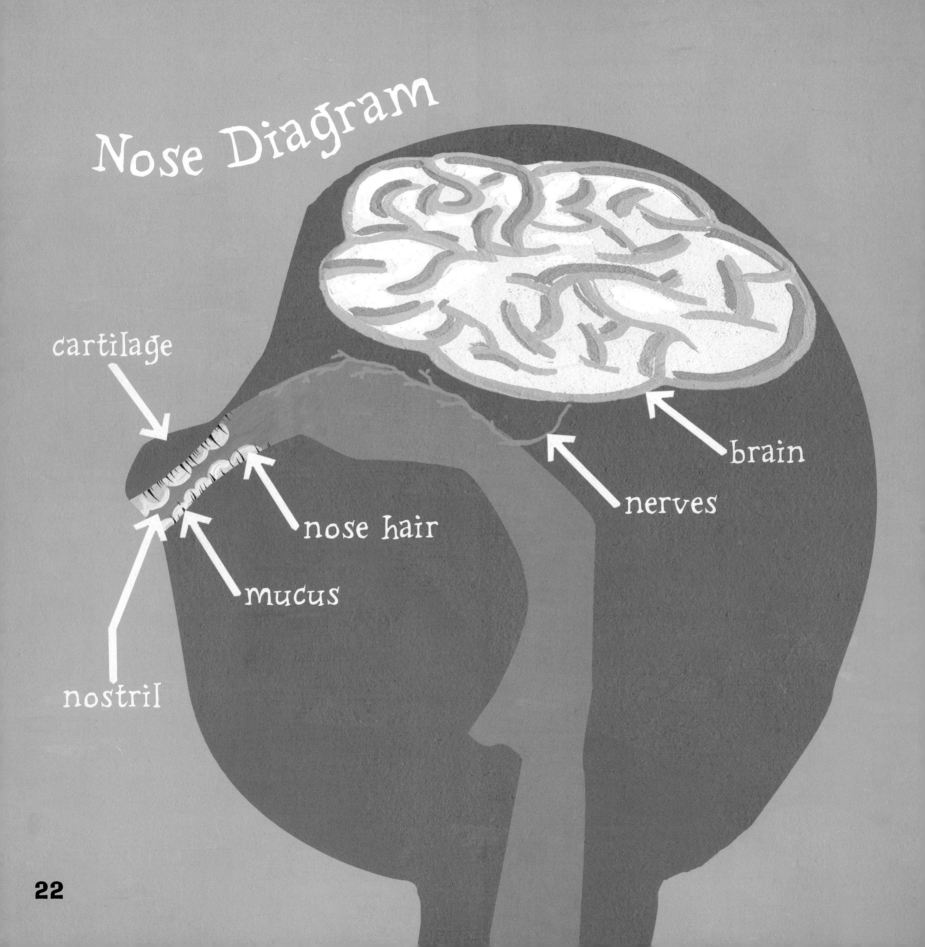

Nose Diagram

cartilage

brain

nerves

nose hair

mucus

nostril

22

Fun Facts

- An elephant uses its nose for more than smelling. It uses its long trunk to pick up objects and suck up and spray water.

- Your nose has an important job when you breathe. It warms and cleans the air before the air travels down to your lungs.

- Only the top part of your nose is made of bone. The lower part is made of cartilage, a softer bone-like material that can bend.

- Dogs know the difference between people by smelling them. Bloodhounds have a very good sense of smell. Rescuers often use bloodhounds to help them find people who are lost.

Glossary

breathe—taking in air and letting out air through your nose

mucus—a sticky substance in your nose that helps trap odors

nerves—cords running through your body that get and give messages to your brain

nostrils—the two holes near the bottom of your nose

odors—smells in the air

To Learn More

At the Library

Cole, Joanna. *You Can't Smell a Flower with Your Ear! All About Your Five Senses.* New York: Grosset and Dunlap, 1994.

Fowler, Allan. *Knowing About Noses.* New York: Children's Press, 1999.

Nelson, Robin. *Smelling.* Minneapolis: Lerner Publications, 2002.

On the Web

FactHound offers a safe, fun way to find Web sites related to this book. All of the sites on FactHound have been researched by our staff. www.facthound.com

1. Visit the FactHound home page.

2. Enter a search word related to this book, or type in this special code: 140481020X

3. Click on the fetch it button.

Your trusty FactHound will fetch the best sites for you!

Look for all of the books in the Amazing Body series:

Bend and Stretch: Learning About Your Bones and Muscles

Breathe In, Breathe Out: Learning About Your Lungs

Gurgles and Growls: Learning About Your Stomach

Look! A Book About Sight

Look, Listen, Taste, Touch, and Smell: Learning About Your Five Senses

Shhhh… A Book About Hearing

Sniff, Sniff: A Book About Smell

Soft and Smooth, Rough and Bumpy: A Book About Touch

Think, Think, Think: Learning About Your Brain

Thump-Thump: Learning About Your Heart

Yum! A Book About Taste